AFTERIMAGES

Afterimages

Poems

Lenore Myers

SIXTEEN RIVERS PRESS

Printed in the United States of America

Published by Sixteen Rivers Press
P.O. Box 640663
San Francisco, CA 94164
www.sixteenrivers.org

LCCN: 2026934314
ISBN: 978-1-939639-45-5

Cover art: Vera Iliatova, *Subterfuge*, 2022, oil on canvas, 30 x 40 in.
Book design: Wayne Smith

for Max

Contents

GALLERY 1: REGARDS TO BALTHUS

GALLERY 2: NEGATIVE SPACE

GALLERY 3: -SCAPES

GALLERY 1: REGARDS TO BALTHUS

Young Girl at the Window

Ghost of a chair, curved
wood. Louis-something.
Insubstantial.
So sparely painted, a bit
of wall shows, like a touch
of breastbone beneath
a blouse. Not really a chair.
And the room is not really
a room, the girl not a girl.
She stands, hands on sill,
window cast slightly
open to whatever's *out*
there: a greening tree,
orange and tan country
houses, yellowish hills,
edges softening in the gray
-blue haze, till houses
and trees are but a puff
at the center of the canvas:
The window will never
be wider than this!
And the breeze—isn't
there a breeze? Drifting
among the elm leaves,
blousy scent of lilac
at the window sill,
paying no mind to where
things should (or
shouldn't) be, a touch

of blue or a child slipping
in and out of the frame.
While we, we come in
to a room, just looking
for a chair.

Balthus (1908–2001)
Fille à la fenêtre, 1957
63 × 63 3/4 in.
Oil on canvas

Metropolitan Museum of Art of New York

Not currently on view

The Blanchard Children

They are still
children, blanched
in earth
shades. Outsized,
they shroud
the table, floor. Dour
walls enclose
stiff forms. Little
light, no
shared glances.

Thérèse, hard
at work
above the composition
book—her
face, the pages,
blank.

Body
rigid, stretched
canvas.

Something doesn't fit
the boundary, escapes—
barely,
a girl's foot.

Hubert's eye
lidded—or is it

wide
open beneath
the smudge?

In the dark, the eye
wavers—
unsituated, free—
dreams

that coarse,
crumpled sack
behind
the scene.

Balthus (1908–2001)
Les enfants Blanchard, 1937
125 × 130 cm
Oil on canvas

Musée National Picasso-Paris

Purchased from Balthus by Picasso
(a semi-surreal construction)

Still Life

One evening's simple
meal refracted
into reds and blues
and greens, strange
geometries
of what we think
and what we think
we see.
Unremarkable
potato, bread, and water
on a desk meant
for writing. Repast
of an artist,
circles,
rectangles, triangulated
hues
assembled like schoolgirls,
mannerly for the moment—
the chair,
the crockery,
cloth draped
the Dutch way—but
poor, coarse canvas.
Composed
feints:
dull skin prodded
by a fork, a side of boiled
potato vanishes

behind the carafe—or
here,
the execution
of glass decanter
shattered
at the neck. Be it
disobedient
materials or something more
out of hand,
the artist's ire
draws
vessel to joiner's
hammer, makes
a feast of tears.

The cloth, the wall, the table
limned in red—
thrust
of knife point into bread.
And hammer, lying
like an untoward comment
made by one friend
to another,
a little funny and a little
mean. Is the subject
overpainted?

Anyway

one wants to look,

unobtrusive

glass untouched, still

pristine

Balthus (1908–2001)
Still Life, 1937
24.5 × 19 cm
Oil on panel

Wadsworth Atheneum in Hartford, Connecticut

As an art reviewer said:

"Hammer and knife have done their foul work;
the dinner table, in better times . . .
an arena of civilized exchange,
now a ruin and a wreck."

Thérèse Dreaming

Scene
in some disarray,
its unfortunate
furnishing, the eye
in its studied
indifference.
Someone's pawned
vases, upright, still
unbroken.
A cheap brown bench,
chipped. Portrait
of a room dominated
by subterranean
tones, unearthed. Here,
the cloth, crumpled,
as yet unstained. The table,
again, the bare
suggestion of chair,
of legs,
of seat. Unconscionable
turquoise, restless
on the pillow. I, too,
turn my face,
turn to muted
blue, almost lost
in bunched cloth.
Diminished
blue, retreating
to the underside

of thigh, fugitive
as childhood—what
of that? Gaze
seeking the buried
eye, evading
its disrobing. The
most penetrative
vision falters before
those lids, sealed
to prying.
Whatever
is behind the looking
away, the mind
finds its own,
open,   bloom.

Balthus (1908–2001)
Thérèse rêvant, 1938
59 × 51 in.
Paint on canvas

The Metropolitan Art Museum of New York

Once subject to petition for removal

Thérèse on a Bench Seat

Thérèse on the bench seat
tilts, one hand
lifting,

pulls
from her black plaid skirt
centimeter by centimeter,

frees
a single, slender
thread.

Shadow
behind her—depth's
silent

accomplice. Rapt
in Peter Pan collar and white
knee-highs,

Thérèse on the bench seat
illuminates
the ochre dark. In perfect captivity

of the moment,
one could forget
war is coming,

then marriage at nineteen,
and illness, and . . . but no!
Her red sweater says,

"*Attendez!*"
The canvas hangs on
her slipping-

down socks, crumpled
collar, slipping-up
skirt, her

every fiber, caught.
Alarming
to see

that unrelenting
tug at a fragile
strand,

a little criminal to want
to pull.
Only eleven years

remain.
Inside the frame,
she lies

beyond
here, now,
drawing the thread

endlessly, bright
wisp
of thread,

tenuous,
against the dark,
unfinished—

Balthus (1908–2001)
Thérèse sur une banquette, 1939
72.7 × 91.9 cm
Paint on canvas

Last seen in public at auction

For almost sixty years
displayed
on a Beverly Hills
designer-red wall—
made the sweater,
the schoolgirl
skirt, pop

The Victim

My artist enters through the broken door.
Hands tremble, touching brushes, rags.
(But never me. No.) Still cigarette-long, thin,
a voice like ash—when he bothers to speak.
He sets the pitcher on the table, drops
the cloth. The palette is prepared. We'll watch
him re-work—
                                        oh! What monstrosity is this?
Some unclothed woman? Girl? Propped, headless, gray,
askew as if discarded? Or lost?
Not me. I never sat for anything like this.
Those arms, those legs—something isn't right.
Body pitched, rough at the edges, bare
sheet fraying . . . ?
                                                            My artist turns pale,
grips his stomach, bends. He is not well.
He carried men across the line at Maginot
—what was left of men. Every night
the dead returned, mute, gaping. Every night
he screamed awake, a mess of tears and sweat,
till one day he, too, stepped wrong: C*lick*, he stopped—
slag blasted guts: another caught the brunt.
Moaning on the field, *"Oh, my angel—"*
            Angel! He thought his vision was of me!
"My little angel," was what he'd said—me,
who twisted Hubert's arm until welted,
red, his face like crumpled paper—*"O! O!"*
—I never said that I was sorry. Oh,
my brother, I was, I am. An angel,

Hubert—he'll stay beside me to the end.
"The past remains within us, an affliction,"
my artist says now. An affliction.
Is this what I've become? He sees himself
in everything. My little artist, victim
of a force that's broken all of us to pieces—
Blow men and violins to bits, but leave
the trees, the country in its silence, green
and golden, velvet stillness of the hills.
A life I never knew.
                    And what of this
posed body, blush abandoning its soft,
sweet hull, breasts and thighs
mottling under loamy browns and grays?
My artist draws the knife upon the floor,
extends the handle past the frame—me, you,
accuses? Her arms stretch up, unresisting.
She does not touch me, no. What, that morbid
tangle—? Nothing like *my* body! And yet,
that face—gray, like a sickness in his brush
emerges, heavy lidded, blotched as if
with filth and rain . . . Don't turn away, please, don't
go. Forget this stiffening body, face
an afterthought: Don't let this be my own—

Balthus (1908–2001)
La Victime, 1939–46
132 × 218 cm
Paint on canvas

A privately held grief

The Guitar Lesson

The teacher has thrown a girl over her lap.

I had no money, nothing. I was alone against the world. I did everything to live, from painting chairs to translating. I painted The Guitar Lesson *to cause a scandal. It was the only way of getting attention.*

The guitar has been tossed to the floor.

It worked well. Too well.

The teacher has grabbed the girl's hair with one hand.

Because of that show I met Artaud and Picasso, Miró, Giacometti, Derain. I started to make money from portraits, my monsters.

The teacher has pulled her head back.

The theme is a mere pretext.

The teacher's other hand grips the girl's bare thigh.

Painting is dead. Painters are less interested in painting than in expressing their personality. If you have personality, the best thing you can do is get rid of it.

The girl's black skirt is thrown back.

The perversity is in your eyes. Not the painting.

The girl's vulva is exposed.

It is not a question of what I like. If you paint, you must leave your ego behind.

Maybe you like to do to audiences what the teacher is doing to the girl.

I believe in the image. When I paint the image, it's like a prayer. I believe in prayer.

To whom do you pray?

To God, naturally.

For whom do you paint?

I feel the light which is God, and my mind and my hand are merely machines which listen. You listen to what you've got to do.

The girl yanks at her teacher's dress.

Painting helps me to live, gives me strength. Painting is living. I have always taken or left things according to my needs.

The teacher's breast is exposed, nipple erect.

My hand did what it had to do.

The teacher has the artist's face.

Balthus (1908–2001)
La Leçon de guitar, 1934
and various interviews with the artist

Ownership unacknowledged

The artist's altercations with her alter-self

Thérèse

She's composed now,
just a girl in an adult
chair, sunk in
the room, her face
a sallow window
on a closed
interior. Her gaze
brushes past
you, and me,

        self forgotten
        as a dream. Electric
        illusion of slight
        hand resting lightly
        on the knee—ah,

glossy pink
remnant of brush
stroke at her cheek.
But the canvas
is really board—

        turning
        green and sour,
        acidic in disrepair.
        Still, life might be
        captured

in this narrow room,
manipulations
of light and shadow
and color, convincing
the mind you can touch.

Balthus (1908–2001)
Thérèse, 1938
39 1/2 × 32 in.
Oil on cardboard mounted on wood

Somewhere in the basement of the Met

The Painting of *André Derain*

In this room, nothing
stands between you
and your art. Nothing.
The door is cracked open.
Beyond this room lies
another, anonymous, dark.
        While you work, a woman
sits, exposed, slightly
smiling. You have lifted her
skirt, lowered her shirt. Her
mouth is satisfied. Unlike
the door, her eyes are
closed. She is having an idea
about something that isn't
in this room, a fantasy. I
cannot stop now to interpret
her silence!
        A great man who has slipped
his left ring finger inside
his garment stands before you.
The other hand awaits
his task. A creation
nearly as fine as the woman's
nipples: the pupils
of his eyes.
        Masterful. He appeared,
gravid and expansive
as a planet,
while you worked. His bodily presence

is undeniable. And yet,
propped atop that mountainous frame,
a squared-off ovoid
with eye bags
sulks, that scowling crown
of genius, as if
he's about to conduct an opera
above your head,
his brow high,
creased, like the arms of a *T*,
its stem his nose, thick
as a man's body, and hung—
        Turned-down thin lips purse:
sacred, a monument to sacrifice,
his mien a victory
underscored by the knife edge
of his well-ironed collar.
        The Artist: He has come.
Your floor is swept bare.
Your frames are up against the wall.
Your canvases are stretched and nailed.

Balthus (1908–2001)
André Derain, 1936
112.7 × 72.4 cm
Oil on wood

Somewhere in the basement of the mind

Mother, 1972 and 2010

Arm up, shielding
yourself—
            deflated
diaphragm
sulks between ribcage
crests

Yoko Ono sunglasses
       flash on
(what we can see of)
        your face

I'd wanted to be out of focus
        and

in Dad's dilating
      eye

only revealing a certain aspect

Like a Weston bell pepper
        all glossy
                  undulation

in the nude sessions

Wearing only an antique muff—

How polite

women

used

to warm their hands!

you laughed—

between your hip bones

Harold Myers, Jr. (1927–2005)
Untitled, 1972
4 × 5 in.
Gelatin silver photograph in a gold-painted faux–Art Deco frame

Currently in my bedroom closet

Did you ever see, do you remember,
how much your parents were once in love?

GALLERY 2: NEGATIVE SPACE

Mother, 1975

She's looking at the camera,
mostly—eyes slightly
   shifted
to something just outside
              the frame. She said it
was me,
but we don't see
me, just
   a pile of leaves.

Did my father try to capture
the half-glance

(sensing the something)

the soft pink
    slip
of eye—the divided

moment of her?

Harold Myers, Jr. (1927–2005)
Untitled, 1975
5 × 7 in.
Photo print on matte paper

In a long-disused file cabinet in a storage unit

Pop Art No. 5

Big black and ugly

your threatening
monumental

slab

towering heaps
of glazed cylinders
    rough thrown and
sliced

Visiting school-
children
at Seattle Art Museum

   broke
into tears
         at the sight

Baroque Vase

Like you'd cast your own
loosely thrown
     -together
self
         into those precariously stacked black
      glazed hollows—

seemingly about to come crashing—

anyway you traded that piece

("visceral, risk-taking . . .")

for weed

We could've

Baroque into Tears
when it was gone!

you old terror
you

broke vase

*

Over the crowd of serious craftsmen, the potters—their shouted *NO*'s—
it was 1960-something and in your black turtleneck and beard you WERE

the *SHOCK* of the NEW—you said:

What the ARTIST makes
his objects OF

paint slabs or drips or burnt cigars or barrettes or thrown or punched or mangled clay or

is not important

but the amount of TRUTH

in it

*

I was a girl and my dreams started
sprouting holes

Whatever was going on at that dream moment would just
slip
in
to
the
hole
in-
(O!)
-cluding me
stuck I
couldn't
pull
myself
out

Like a lovely dream a family
trip to Disneyland

somewhere outside Anaheim
the motel its dark
faux-wood panels and narrow
mirrored halls
lined in worn polyester
carpet of velveteen ochre and rust

    decorated with ornate fleur-de-lis
splash stains and a smattering
   of burn holes

For a handful of coins
  breakfast rattled
    from the machine
cold milk thunked
  and a box of frosted
flakes stuck
        in the coils
  when your agitated
voice twisted
  down the hall
down the
  long column of glassy black you were
    shouting
  you were losing
it
 I started shaking
the machine   hitting
the glass
  but nothing
    fell down   I
    reached up   trying
  to shove
my arm into the mouth
    of the machine like it was another
self-sized hole

*

Maybe form's a kind
of in-
  florescent
beauty or expression of
  implicit
meaning maybe hidden
  from its maker tucked within a difficult—
meaning hard to face—
reality

and the past
the difficult
  beauty
of the past

its inelegant contours
  become smoothed in memory
(meaning become lies)

*

  Late nights
returning home herringbone
sport coat suffused
  with pipe tobacco and kiln
  emanating
a kind of mineral
  sweetness

(with just a
  whiff
of inferno)

We lived with the difficulty of your being
you —a geologic pressure
secretly intensifying
under all that forced
normativity

Next morning your jacket
neat on its hall door hanger
and a personal effect
lying
on the dining room table—
but this "memory"
is really second-hand

*

Dancing lightly through
the scorched field
of your life its work
proof that our doings
and undoings
and self-undoings
twist for years
through the lives of others

Making something
of a parent's failings—
one of life's great
unfairnesses— a fortunate task

*

Pop! Let's take a page from *Life* magazine:

busily scissoring—

Background, blurred:

nudie pic & poster, a two-toned grinning sunburst

Below, the foreground: here goes

your '62 VW Bug—

dented & white   (but for one green door)

careening through a cartoon desert

past a Japanese pagoda & that go-go girl on the dunes

swim-shimmying her brains out

On the upper horizon, the main subject:

pipe-smoking professor   rakish, unbuttoned

shirt   (midnight rages

hidden

behind the half-smirk

& salt & pepper beard)

Coming in fast at 10 o'clock: a fleet

of black & white B-52's—

ready the f-bombs . . .

(roar of approval)

Pop! Here's our mutual hot mess, our military-industrial rebel-art complex

*

In living with and seeing you

now only

in your work I

almost know myself
one small part of a series

*

My mother got your last good
art joke

Found you blotchy and bloated from drink
salvaged
Heap
from the post-divorce wreckage

Heap
still sits on her living room floor
like a big pocked ceramic pile
of cow manure

Years later my little boy would scoot
by and drop
Cheerios and toy trucks
down its volcanic mouth

*

What the ARTIST *makes her objects* OF

old cereal and bartered art kiln char of recurring dreams

is not important

but the amount of

TRUTH

all our sliced and stacked and severed black
holes

in it

Harold Myers, Jr. (1927–2005)
Baroque Vase, 1965
and
Lenore Myers (b. 1974)

Posthumous collaboration
of a lost work
in glazed ceramic

partly reconstructed
in black print
on acid-free paper

and secondhand smoke

(Certainly not an homage)

I Remember

I remember summer the dads in white t-shirts lighting rockets in clear glass bottles, holding the bottles as far out as they could as the fuses burnt down. I remember a dad, his weathered face, his squint through sparks and smoke. I remember the fuses snapped and barked in his face before he looked away.

I remember pulling down a limb of the loquat tree, plucking from it a small fruit. I remember prying it apart, juice streaking lines through the dirt on my hands.

I remember children walking along the sidewalk, pointing, laughing.

I remember my mother showing me how to use a toothpick to crush insect eggs hiding among the prickles.

I remember the large ivory towel wrapped around her body, another turbaned on her head.

I remember the bright main bedroom of our house made into a studio, blank, freshly stretched canvases leaning against a wall, the easel with a half-finished painting of a nightmarish open door, and the oily whites and blacks and blues and reds on the mixing paper smelling minerally and good.

I remember the bird flying white over the bottlebrush lifting like a letter on the breeze across the ditch and beyond the train tracks. I remember being grateful for that, and also sad.

I remember my mother's greenhouse.

I remember her big cheekbones and her strong jaw and her straight, well-defined nose.

I remember lumpy succulents like speckled rocks, and rows and rows of cacti, their spiny rosettes, some with white gossamer filament threading criss-crossed spines.

I remember a warm trickle down my leg, pooling at my feet. I remember a dark, wet path making its way toward the sidewalk.

I remember the bathroom turned into a darkroom.

I remember a fistful of sparklers, thick clouds of sulphur stink going up my nose.

I remember piercing a tiny, white cocoon until it collapsed and splotched red. I remember being surprised by that.

I remember the white-brightness and heat and the salt tang of my own lips when I licked them.

I remember my parents slow-dancing in the living room at night. I remember the lamp suspended above, my mother's brown hair flaming auburn, sunset.

I remember my dad running into the living room shouting, *Fire!*

I remember the fruit was more than half-seed. I remember consuming every last bit of musky orange flesh. I remember wanting more.

I remember setting matches to firework worms.

I remember standing in the yard, watching her through the glass as she chased the last bird out the door.

I remember how they glowed orange and their black ash bodies smoked and crawled in the gutter and twisted and smoked until spent.

I remember black garbage bags taped over the windows and the sharp, vinegary smell of developer in the bathtub. I remember other chemicals in plastic tubs on a white linoleum countertop crazed with gold, and it was so dark I could hardly see the countertop or the gold or even my own face in the mirror.

I remember her heavy brow and her hooded eyes.

I remember the smell of fire retardant in the garage. It was heavily sweet, like too much cherry candy.

I remember that smell mixing with the piney odor of turpentine.

I remember that she was beautiful as she picked me up and carried me back into the house.

Burnt cherry candy.

I remember barely being able to see the sparklers through the smoke and tears. I remember coughing over and over and wondering, was this supposed to be fun?

I remember the following days looking at the power lines across the train tracks behind our house and wondering if my birds were perched there right now.

I remember turning around to see my mother opening the black iron gate, hurrying toward me.

I remember standing in the driveway.

I remember the rotating lights and the flashes white-red-white against our garage door.

I remember jumping up to open the sliding glass door and trying to chase out my loose parakeets.

I remember the *shik-shak* of the shovel when my mother stomped on it as she dug a hole in the ground.

I remember the rocket shooting crazy fast and hitting the garage door and flipping up and over and onto the roof and the dads stampeding up our driveway through the side gate shouting as they ran.

I remember my mother running in from the backyard hollering, *Get out! Get out of the house!*

I remember thinking I never wanted to leave home.

Joe Brainard (1942–94)
I Remember (1970)

Remix, replay

Summertime (2010) in Slemani

The gun—first I'd heard
in months—*pop pop pop*
and the dog, frenzied,
and the woman, screaming
for a while,
and sirens, and yelling, and more screaming,
now indistinct
in the very dark.

Shadows crouch behind
my room's cheap furnishings,
the night wailing itself to sleep.
You are awake and ready,
and there is nothing to be done.

In the painting Summertime*, the dreamer lies*
outstretched in a blood-red jacket
in the field beneath the mountain.

Above her, the massif face,
severe. Shadows beneath the rocks
undercut dark troughs to spite the day.

Some nights here, the mountain's indifferent,
towering whiteness fills the dream field,
pure, barren, cretaceous. Tender within
its walled compound, the body
craves forgiving ground, wraps
its jacket tighter—

*

Morning. I might breathe a little better
in the country beyond the concrete
where mountains' sheer faces
begin to sharpen.

In this country within a country—
autonomous, guarded—
I drive past modest dwellings,
flat rooftops
spiked with mantid weaponry,
past the checkpoint,
into smuggler's foothills
and the haze of surrounding mountains,
past men washing cars in glacial waters—
I drift along the surface of the valley
alongside lengths of wooly white foam,
white froth at a boundary of green.

Park, hike up the mountain
overlooking the valley. There, perched
improbably on a rock-strewn hillside,
sentinel goats, brown, shaggy, and horned
(one examines me with its alien yellow eye—shakes its head).

The boulders make me gasp and struggle—
massive rocks, bulwarks
as if pushed down by a giant
against prying hands, peering eyes.
Finding my footing,
I clamber up the boulders tumbled along the glacial stream

that sluices from a crevasse
knifed into the hillside—slip, trip,
plunge into icy waters
(even the mountains gasp).
Hauling out, strip my sodden clothes—
this is absolutely forbidden—
spread them to dry midstream
on the warm bone-table of the mountain.
Cold, wet, I sit.
Maybe I shouldn't have come here.
What more is there to see? Rocks, huge ones,
some unclimbable, the churning ice-melt, skies
as featureless here as on any other side of Earth?
Have I come this far only to fall
like a dumb pebble to the bottom
of a freezing pool?
Toe the water—slaps the nerves.
The stream babbles like an old man
overspilling with memories—
shouldn't I stay and listen,
even not knowing the language?
Lowering into icy clearness, willingly
a fool, losing my senses, happily
unseen in this secluded theater, at play
in ever-pouring, companionable racket.

The boulders begin to darken.
The sun is slipping.
Eventually the water numbs my extremities
and the clothes must go back on.
I stumble back down the mountain,
return to the clatter of rusted trucks,

the stench of diesel,
the jeers and shouts of passing men,
pull over, and stand
between two broad lanes of highway
on the wide hellstrip.

Now at some distance from the mountains, I can see
rough notches in a smooth, vertical face—
small, dark mouths gape in the rock—
some say rebels hid here from MiGs and tanks,
plotted suicidal retributions.
Now they are crumbling,
graffitied hideouts, sheltering teens
too young to remember the war.
They escape ever-watchful elders
to smoke and neck in ancient redoubts.

But I am in the road, and a not-quite form—
nonsensical, what the mind can do
so far from home! —an enormous figure stands,
shaggy as a long-haired goat,
its canid coat filthy, in yellowed clumps,
shedding what little's left of the Kurdish spring.
Ears peak, wolf-like eyes blink—
it turns to gaze after the other
bleating creatures that roam
the open field confettied
with red and yellow wildflowers.
White teeth ribboned over with tongue,
the once-white mass of canine
is moving—Oh, how it moves!
—ambling, loping

so gracefully and toward me,
clumps like grotesque cheese curds
sway and smack against
its body, its predatory
perfection, hurtling
into the decreasing space between us—

*

Later in the night, this time *ratatatatatat*
—hypnic jerks rattle, the mind
in fever-crackle: the death-charge
drives dreams to ground.

No screams. No sirens.

Morning of my departure, I notice
the entrance to the compound
beyond the armed guards' hut—
the roses, staked,
nod in the breeze,
row upon row of well-tended
heads: pink, yellow, red.

Again on the solitary highway,
and the young man turns from the wheel—
I hate this place—
I hate it—
They can't make me fight!
I have an uncle in Canada—
I'm leaving—
I'm leaving—

I'm leaving as soon as I can

*

Summertime. *Night slips across the sky, the hillocks below*
mounded in mismatched peaks like verdant breasts

The mountain slumbers

The dreamer
roused from sleep—miles to unfold, striding
across the field, over rises and falls

Her jacket flutters in her wake—
so red, it hums!

Racing
to a constantly receding horizon

The fabric, worn thin, begins to tear,
the ground no longer holds—

She is almost out of breath
She has almost fled the painting

Lenore Myers (b.1974),
memory of Slemani, 2010
and
Balthus (1908–2001),
Summertime (1935)
The Mountain (1936-37)

At the Met Fifth Avenue, or in storage

In Slemani, as in the painting,
Summertime was revised
into *The Mountain.*

Maybe it had never really been
summer in the first place?

Memory of that time frayed,
was overlaid, became
another land.

I could imagine belonging there.

On "Elizabeth Bishop and the Management of Distance"

I. "Cirque d'Hiver"

For about two years, I have been not writing "Elizabeth Bishop and the Management of Distance." It is an essay, some thoughts on how beginning to talk to someone in a low voice from across the room while slowly moving toward them, perhaps in a sidelong manner and while looking at something else, can result in an impression of intimacy—if only by contrast with a seeming coolness and impersonality.

Across the floor flits the mechanical toy,
fit for a king of several centuries back.
A little circus horse with real white hair.
His eyes are glossy black.
He bears a little dancer on his back.

The question of purpose hovered at the start, indicating that more preparation was needed.

So, I read letters written by and to Bishop. I traveled from coast to coast. I read critical studies of her development as a writer (often of an overly—to my mind—psychoanalytic variety). I lost my apartment. I read scholarly analyses of her poems, spent a lot of money, read drafts and unpublished work, read informal recollections of those who knew her. I was unsettled for the better part of two years. I went overseas, left my books behind I was so in love, stored forty-two boxes of books, I so wanted a home, shipped some boxes, lost them, lost a great love I lost then found then lost . . . continued to study Bishop's words.

She stands upon her toes and turns and turns.

Bishop's poems render emotional depths beneath initially unremarkable surfaces, yet they perplex in their sometimes disinterested or detached tone.

A slanting spray of artificial roses
is stitched across her skirt and tinsel bodice.
Above her head she poses
another spray of artificial roses.

Her careful, direct language and almost clinically precise description amplifies the object of attention as if under an enlarger. Yet the occasion for speaking—the motive behind the speaker's attention—is, at first, hard to pin down—*Why is she telling me this, now?*

His mane and tail are straight from Chirico.
He has a formal, melancholy soul.

The thought is hardly original to me—many have remarked Bishop's oblique strategies in getting to the heart of the matter. But her effacements remain intriguing, attractive—as if she were speaking to me but with her back turned, and I have to lean in and listen closely to catch the drift of her low tones. Of her face I can see only her upswept hair, the line of her jaw, the side of her full cheek, maybe a bit of eyelash.

He feels her pink toes dangle toward his back
along the little pole

Maybe, while she busies herself straightening figurines on a shelf, I might sidle behind, re-tuck a wisp of her hair, wrap my arms around her waist, press myself against her, murmur, *Stay, stay.*

that pierces both her body and her soul

She runs a finger along a book's spine . . .

and goes through his, and reappears below,
under his belly, as a big tin key.

I love her terribly, hopelessly, resolutely.

II. Questions of Winter

It begins to occur to me as I continue not to write "Elizabeth Bishop and the Management of Distance" that it is a naive optimism to think that anything about distance is at all manageable—for instance, distance from home (not having one), distance from achievement of one's academic and professional goals (not realizing them), distance from the beloved (four years and now half a planet)—and worst of all, distance, at times, from who I take myself to be.

He canters three steps, then he makes a bow,
canters again, bows on one knee,

(Who *do* I take myself to be?)

canters, then clicks and stops, and looks at me.

Being an otherwise resilient, resourceful, and practical woman (this sounds good for the moment, let's go with it), I am attempting to approach "Elizabeth Bishop and the Management of Distance" in small increments. Now that I have a young child, I am practicing breaking things down for him into small pieces whenever he is overwhelmed by the large. *Don't worry*, I say, *You don't have to do it all at once. You can start with just this one: the plainest, squarest wooden block of the bunch . . .*

I am so reassuring when I speak of how to handle the blocks: the mother's voice, like shelving. I am often alone with my son, and I talk to myself. Breaking things down for him. For us.

But now the whole project seems stuck on a bad premise. Didn't Bishop spend her own life's work not so much managing distance as suffering it, re-creating it, maintaining it, and, ultimately, aestheticizing its painful consequences?

The dancer, by this time, has turned her back.

Or, *seemingly* painful consequences—was it always so, for her?

For didn't Bishop choose to restrain her poem's affections, choose to delay her visits with friends until they broke down, were sent to sanitariums, married women who weren't her? Didn't she dream of drinking alone by the wavering blue flame, in an artichoke-green shack teetering on the edge of the northeastern seaboard, grudgingly connected to land by just one long, frayed extension cord? What did she say to Lota in Brazil that she could not bring herself to say in any poem? What in that cool breast did she reveal that was flowing, has flown, will always be unknown to anyone, unknown by me?

My own confessions of limitation and failure, my self-doubts, my little series of come-to-nothings, are revealed to an unblinking page. It is not especially like a lover, although some receptivity is involved.

He is the more intelligent by far.

I type my come-to-nothings as if gazing into the open face of Love. In him, all my nothings resolve into delightful, immediate, and concrete *presence*. This is also known as "text." The process of making it is much less like lovemaking than I care to admit.

Facing each other rather desperately—

his eye is like a star—

How do I turn such bright absence into small, square blocks? Not much bigger than, say, the space above the seat of an ordinary breakfast room chair. Once my beloved and I sat for an hour, silent, holding hands. We were suffused, each radiant in the presence of the other. Now, I can't imagine less light than this. I cannot bear his life-sized absence.

we stare and say, "Well, we have come this far."

Elizabeth Bishop (1911–79)
"Cirque d'Hiver," 1940
and **Lenore Myers** (b. 1974)
Assemblage (posthumous collaboration)

I've recovered (what I can)
from those years
and piles of books and papers.

And when the books were shipped
and "lost"
by the Richmond (California or Virginia?)
mail-sorting facility
I began to brood and build: re-creations.

Potsherd

Of the amphora on my desk: Most of it
lies in dust and shards. Yet I loved
not only what was broken
but also what survived.
                    So I salvaged
the beauty of shoulders—held, barely
raised, as by a breath—
above the sharp, undulating edge
of the abyss I'd struck into its body.

Your hands had wrought a shape,
and fire fixed it;
but firing made its nature new
and secret. Then hands and heart grew
stranger—
    unmade in an instant.

Harold Myers, Jr. (1927–2005)
Untitled, 1985

Collected shards

But we hold this treasure in earthen vessels
—Paul, 2 Corinthians 4:7

As Jay DeFeo Paints *Deathrose/The White Rose/The Rose* (1958–66)

1

Did daily attention to paint
its weight
its hues in changing light
its sculptural bulges
chasms
make your painting
more
like words

2

I start in the figure
as you never did
although the surface was of immediate concern
you started in the thing

itself   paintbrush
between your teeth

3

What defines a figure

Who says what ground

The art of FUNK

            The surface all fucked up

  or

The process of fucking
up into revelation

4
You break it the
surface
never lies
right with you

5
By weight, scale, undercuts, nearly no color, centripetal
form and sheer
physical *work*

To *MAKE* a surface

(Circles and triangles on bare canvas)

STAND
a visual *body*
of labor

6
But first, the painting
suspended
like a saint on the artist's apartment wall

The paint grows heavier and heavier

The canvas groans

Morning argument of drill set and knife

The wall sighs and sags

The artist scraping down again   down
            to the supports

7
Today   the brush
strokes light
along petals

8
Tomorrow
the knife takes
it all
down
to canvas and powder

9
Dust so thick you can't see
    the end of your marriage—

Paintbrush clenched between teeth

10
Get it all
the way down
to the supports

Ground
of some kind
of spiritual   relief
in eighteen spokes

11

Star beacon   Blade array   *Deathrose*

Oil plywood mica beads copper wire barrettes

Set against dark matter
of the world
the Old World

Laid on thick O my
two-thousand-pound splintered halo

Light screaming in, the painting a terrible radiance
  Manichean annunciation of petal and gouge, black
    undercut by white—

In the city where it was made—
men roll dice on the corner, patrols toss
 batons, someone
  lies
forgotten under the bridge, children
 laugh in an empty lot

Click lifts the revolver, the Panther crouches

The paint is lead
The city clenches its teeth: 1964

12

Eruption!   or sudden bloom
like the first hot spill

Confluence of petals
profusion of curlicues

Atop the ladder the artist, knife
in teeth then
in hand and
cutting
like a surgeon
into the gleam of sclera

The paint pulls back   un-folding   *The*
          White Rose

13
O congealing starry O Big Bang O my stony outcropping

Now stretching more canvas   nailing
on more wood, it is
threatening
collapsing under its own

Eight-year concatenation
    of paint   too heavy
for cotton duck canvas and that
unfathomable center
   drooping
accelerating
   into origin   limpid smack-suck of time

14

Petals sag   the figure
that onetime act of dilation

suspended—

15

In the wake of eight years bent laddered spattered and
broke the studio floor
encrusted

The tearing *back* and *down* of the thing

Knives sharpened on drill sets

Into the silent apertures

16

As if to fix an ephemeral
image
of presence

17

Or raise a moment
against its passing

18

(Dropped

words
wrenches
a clatter of artless)

And the whole thing . . . from a scratch

19

You were broke and wouldn't let it go
so
for years the gallery bought those gallons of white paint

That's ok
words aren't really free either

20

It's a question of perspective—

Seeing art and its costs
personally

I never get lines how I want them

21

But painting is over now

Ripped down   forklifted out

Loaded onto a Ryder truck

(i.e., *The Rose*)
went out the window
took the wall with it

(Jay evicted from her apartment, 1966)

22
And what that paintbrush carried
rots the teeth

A kind of palsy—

Like walking on the back of a whale

23
The writer brushes away the word-scrapings

No, and *no*, and *no*

The rent is overdue   Fog over
Pine Street
    crumbles at the edges

Eight years
      in the dustcrowd—
            whispering in my ear

Turn
            and—
  the poem, waiting
            like a mother.

How I will miss her!

24
In this room, I put up
  words—pictures—
   and take them down again.

Putting up. Taking down.

To amuse myself I
break
        the frames

My son asks
   why
I say *To make*
    the devils fall

25
No one asked
What would you give up for art?

It's just a process, your—

Folded in   scraped down

Then gathered
like broken branches and bruised fruit

Or standing day in day out
like Schiller at his desk

huffing rotten apples

Painting over now

Jay long dead and *The Rose*
in slow decay

flecks of paint and bits of plaster flake

the etch remains

26
Walking after the first rain

Drifts of blossoms
smudge concrete

an open window
a little boy's laughter

patter of tumbling apples

Jay DeFeo (1929–89)
The Rose, 1958–66
Oil paint with fabric, printer paper, string,
toner, and wood on life-sized canvas

Once worked into a wall
of an apartment home, cut out,
trucked to a museum in Pasadena,
hauled to the Art Institute
of San Francisco, only
to disappear
behind another wall, crumbling.

Re-homed at the Whitney
Museum of American Art.

Too many of us torn
from the sites of our original installation.

GALLERY 3: -SCAPES

At the Window

Inscrutable tangle
of fir and thicket, almost
concealing the barn
across the field, those greens
and golds of nearly summer
and the single door, barely
visible—here,
she's partway out
the window, half-
way to the world
beyond the sill. She reclines
headfirst into the green,
one thick leg
braced upon the chair, good
and bare for climbing up and out
and running far . . .
                                        But no,
most of her remains
in here, cramped
and cool and gray, so gray
it dulls the blouse, the hair.
Why linger in a room
so cold and narrow?
                              Outside the window
grows a world resinous
and evergreen, deepening
its roots, the shrubbery
with its newly yellow
shoots, the tumultuous

thicket, virtually unseen—oh
let it be my own, the distant barn,
the waiting door, quit
this patient, unnatural wondering!

Balthus (1908–2001)
Jeune fille à la fenêtre, 1955

Another private (re)collection

The painting an inadvertent,
momentary
biography of the writer

Portrait of the Space Where the Portrait of the Child Would Be

This is the space where the portrait of the child would be

What's so bad about making someone's portrait

I'm his parent I'm already part of the making every day that's being a parent being the asshole who says "No" or "Do this instead" or sometimes actually letting him be

Why not let the kid be   his own kidness

It's like a Cubist thing
childhood
a moment always
in motion and the beauty of that

Why try to nail the kidness down

Between the child's unself-
consciousness
and emerging social self
            the self looking
in and on itself

He's not a project or a concept he's   an actual kid
let him emerge   himself

Trying to
capture him in a moment or
wanting to
is not wrong

Himself is his own book to write

Captivating
the being emergent
from childhood its growth   its self-creating
freedom drove
Balthus   drives you
to capture
those moments of self-creation

Self-creation is not being a page in someone else's book

I never wanted to be a page in someone else's book

I wanted to be my own horse even while weeping enormous horse-tears

We should tell the story together someday

Weeping bobbing my anvil head I promise we will find the time to tell the story together

I promise

I hope it's not too late

Soon you'll be done with being a child

And the horse tears will be your own

And you will weep your very own page

L. Myers (b. 1974)
Notebook excerpt, 2025

Study for portrait of artist-mother and child

The Triangular Field

Beyond the hedgerow, just
a scritch, barely human
form, so close to being
landscapey—two triangles
away from serious
grazing sheep, indistinct
as growing grass. Waving
in the solemn green, a blue
someone hailing from
the larger field—calling
another someone—
we'll never know who,
or if they heard. The horse
is grazing comfortably within
the reassuring geometries,
these green, orderly lanes
of light and land. Across
the golden field, aglow
in summer's lengthening, an
apple tree seems to leap
into the light, screaming
beneath her bouffant of leaves—
isn't it usual to see
something a bit wrong?
But leaping is unfolding

life, its nervous squiggles,
in plain sight—here it is
only seeming, and horses,
undisturbed, lack perspective.

Balthus (1908–2001)
Great landscape with trees, 1955
Convolutions of wood pulp daubed with ink

It must be held somewhere?

The Other Horse in *Andrei Rublev*

The essence of life   stumbles
down stairs—steadies   itself
neck out   -stretched stumbles
again—landing right
before the rail
collapses

The essence of life falls   twenty-four frames in
a second—the time it takes
to capture   light

The essence of life was saved
from the butcher
then shot   on camera

The essence of life   never dreamed
how it would end   But you and I can

see it   walk
into the frame   anytime
(how can you not?)

Play it over
and over again

Tarkovsky (1932–86)
Andrei Rublev, 1966

When I'm looking at a horse
I have a feeling I'm in direct contact
with the essence of life itself.
—Tarkovsky

I watch it over and over,
think—
it can't be real.
The more I watch, the less I feel.

It's make-believe!
No. It's real.

I love to watch movies!

But this flick—
call it *snuff*—
feels sicker and sicker.

Perspective with a Pen

I.

Sometimes art seems ridiculous
beyond reason.

I try to imagine its possibility
without faith.

How exactly
is one to proceed?

In plain, living reality
(I suppose).

And "suppose"
becomes an image
reflected
through mind's glassy
curve, cuts
through
the dark, wavers
a moment
on a white wall—

belief
in the act of making
light
of itself.

II.

Daniele Barbaro, his perspective
shaped by science
and ordinary spectacles,
as well as the virtues (with my excisions
and interpolations),
of his own "dark chamber," says:

Close all shutters
and doors until no
light enters . . .
but through the lens,
and opposite hold
a piece of paper. . . . There
on the paper you
see the whole . . .
of earth, its distances,
its colors and shadows,
the motion
of the fleeing herd,
clouds, birds
flying. . . . Holding the paper . . .

III.

Scene in Tarkovsky's *Andrei Rublev*: A ragged man
flees across the river

Untie the rope

In my own mind, as in that scene,
there is a mob

The rope is tangled!

shouting to pull down
a disturbing
idea in patched cloth—its base
burns

Cut the rope

Silks swell, lift
the artist, this ordinary basket of bones—

Cut the rope!

Hot air
makes a silken

bloom

balloon—

I'll show you Cut the rope

And suddenly you are
rising
unrestrained by the certainty of gravity
trussed only in faith
(and rope)
to carry you

The flying machine burns and smokes—
a massive censer

swinging
over Earth

I fly!

IV.

Gasping
over the incensed mob
at this unnatural height
you can see
marshlands
and scattered trees stripped
by winter you can see
clouds
drifting on the surface of the water
as if drowned
in pools sky
breaking through you
see the whole
herd running in
God's cursive
gleaming
rivers inscribed on smooth
pages of earth

I fly

V.

Inevitably the bloom
drops, the bone bag
deflates
bumps and scrapes

You should choose the glass that does best . . . and . . .

plows
headlong into a small peninsula

As smoke like marsh mist
rises, the artist
lies on the ground, still
bound

. . . cover it but leave
a little in the middle clear

The balloon collapses,
exhales, its failure
warm mist

A horse walks through

and open . . .
you will see
a still brighter affect . . .

Ambles
through the aperture in-
to your dark chamber,
lenses
into being, as if to say
"yes," walks on-
to your white page

Daniele Barbaro (1514–70)
La pratica della perspettiva
(**The Practice of Perspective**), 1568
and
Tarkovsky (1932–86)
Andrei Rublev, 1966

one falls
and remains fallen and one
rolls
and rises

like that other story

do we fall
to live
closer to ground
or
do we remain
fallen
and struggle

until the ground
rises
to meet us

Study for *No. 1 Evening Snow on Mt. Hira*

Only loosely sketched, but somehow all the more
alive, as if directly approaching
the unknown. Behind the foreground—familiar
bones of trees scrape the sides of huddled huts,
the valley ringed by mineral sharpness.
Above the smear of the season's closing storm,
a pale mountain, indistinct, hovers.
The landscape strewn with flurries: compositional
notes, discarded names, perhaps,
or a shopping list for all I know.
Indecipherable characters! Tiny jots
of men and horses haul the remains
of fall, their heads bowed under a recurring
figure—"cold"? Or "mountain"?
Calligraphic signs of the everyday
embellish a pervasive wash of gray;
images wrested free as the rest is frozen,
light, belonging to no world of the flesh.
Am I free? Free as charcoal clouds'
inky wisps, floating above the daily clutter
of aches and twinges—"perhaps a better noun here,"
or "pasta for dinner?"—I rub my belly's boulder, drawn
again to the nearly featureless white mound.
Say the past is just an image, sketched anew
each time you look at it, sheet upon sheet.
And the future, an image
you can't release. Stubborn,
uncharacterized: a mute immanence.
Still, the mountain waits, and still, I hesitate.

Hiroshige (1797-1858)
Study for ***No. 1 Evening Snow on Mt. Hira*** (1834)

Honolulu Museum of Art

I remember the first time I experienced snowfall.
I was in graduate school in Illinois. I met a friend in the brightly lit
football stadium near my apartment.
The night was thick with snowfall!
We ran, laughing, throwing snowballs, delighted and oblivious
as children. I was surprised by the cushioned warmth of the night air.
(Only later did I discover the razor cold of deep winter.)
I remember how my friend laid himself in a thick pile of icy fluff
and swept his long arms and legs up and down, an ungainly snow angel.

Well after we parted, I had a baby. He and his fiancée did, too.
After maybe a year's silence, we talked again, sharing
the messes and joys that were now our lives. Not long after, I learned
my friend had taken his own life.

All these little facts, assembled. And for what?

On Santa Cruz Mountain

When I was ten, my mother left
a daughter in the driveway,
a husband in a haze
of weed, the mind's slow
exhale. Each heart
retreated to its hollow
chamber, its lonely
dissolutions . . .
Was she gone a day? A week?
That summer, my mother left
a muffled stillness in the house.
Though it was summer,
there was no laughter.
I didn't go outside. I walked
dim, stuccoed halls
and newly spartan rooms,
waited
in the kitchen
for something
to happen. I pressed my ear
to the door of the garage:
What is he doing in there?
Sound of a jar rolling
round and round on the floor.

            Why return now? The past
is good as ash, cold,
scattered, dissolving
at the touch. Yet some particle
remains, uncindered—

a granularity working in,
debriding the mind.
That summer,
my mother returned
and left a second time,
took me to live
and work with her
for room and fare
at Deborah's rambling mountain
ranch an hour's crawl
from my new school, up the Black
Road switchbacks, the snaky,
twisting way up Skyline Trail.
            The school bus stops
at summit's top, opens the door—
I drop the last step
into a heat-crinkled world, insect wired.
Kicking dust along dirt-scrambled rocks
through glassy-winged whine,
vigilant for rattlers, I scuff through
the scent of chaparral,
under bay and black oak,
through green feathers
of fennel, their sun-dashed yellow
blooms. Snap their long necks
for the green spring of licorice
on the tongue—sweeter spit.
Atop the road's crest
splays Deborah's dog,
upside down,
lolling in hot blooms
of dust and blond puffs

of clinging undercoat,
tongue slopping
from toothy maw.
Legs twitch, paws flop—
but the play is staged:
watchful, narrowed eyes
unease me, hold me stiff.
Then rolls her muscled mass
upright, panting—
I hesitate, then risk
a head-scritch. She fidgets
my fingers to just the spot. Her skull
not too unlike the mountain—
impenetrable rock
smattered with burrs and fluff.
A sudden shake detonates
a pale penumbra
of fur and earth—
she dashes off.

Chores now. Measure oats,
heave pails from paddock
to paddock: the daily pull
of (almost) belonging there.
I like the clarity
of simple requirements:
knowing what goes where,
being a fit tool for the task.

The foals are last.
Lazing at the rail, I watch
a colt—
my colt—
munch, nose,

bang
the bucket, bob, and
shake
his head, push for more.
I rest my hand on his forehead,
run the long, mislaid lane
sheeting one nostril white
and one eye bright blue. Harley,
Harlequin, a fool's disguise
pressed against my chest.
For your birthday,
Deborah said.
How
to explain I knew
the gift was hollow?
But I loved immediately,
without condition, heedless
of consequences.
            I let drop his errant face, slip
between rails, allow a brush-nibble.
Then brush follows the beast-arc
of red neck, dust clouding up
and all around, dust
never ceasing, curling, sinuous
soil slough of mountain,
its continual abandonment
of land, enveloping
him, my boots, my hands,
gray and hot with earth.
We lean in to my work
and one another. Lazy,
wide hours in summer heat

sweeping long, slow arcs
along ridges. The late summer sky
a great clear thought,
nearly divine in its simplicity. The mountain
turns red; Harley's coat
is beginning to shine.
        The past is given.
What mattered then
doesn't now—so what
to keep close, what
to salvage—what stamps
its shape into my eye—?
Or what, in the telling, breaks
free of halter and lead.
        Three times that summer, helicopters
like great insects on the hunt
buzz the valley, hack up the ridge
through mountain heat, dust, and gravity—
the farmhands run for cover—men
in plaids and cow boots
who strew poison in rodent holes
that would catch a wrong foot,
who find black widows
hunkered in heaps of firewood, strike
snake's heads, machetes
blood-bright as bodies writhe;
men who nail skins to barn doors,
who work and hay and groom horses
so well, scarce themselves.
Eric, Deborah's boyfriend,
bites his pipe, squints at the sun,
mutters, "Immigration," turns

to pitch the hay.
I never wondered why
they hid. Once, José, gold
tooth gleaming behind a rare grin,
opened his calloused hand:
pale pellets. Then plucked a slug
from a bed of wilting violets: *"Feo,*
feo!" Studiously, in my yellow
notepad: "*Feo means slug.*"
Just weeks before, I'd been saving
similarly obscure lives
in my mother's garden.
I cup my newfound *feo*—
eyestalks bend as if in blessing,
touch my palm. Only later
I learn *feo* means *ugly*.
But *feo* survives by feeling
everything.
On the blue bed
one afternoon, reading,
done with school, I heard
a rumble echo
down the hall, coming
louder, thumping,
pounding,
thunder-stagger—
bodies burst
into my bedroom,
Deborah falling
to the floor, Eric
tumbling behind her—
Don't let him—!

she crawls,
he growls, jerks
her jeans cuff,
she grabs comforter
to counter, pulls
it down, herself up
on my bed.
Eric yanks, yells.
Book vised
in hand, voice going
strange,
I growl—*Get out.*
By her hair now,
he pulls her. And me—
my arm—she grabs,
she squeezes—
Don't let him—
tighter—*hurt me*—
wails—
Don't you love me—?
I am stony, certain
now, entirely strange:
Get out of my room.
Eric, clawing
fierce-clinging fingers
from my arm—*Out,*
now—! Eric lunges,
grabs arms, drags
Deborah, kicking,
across the floor—
a rip—
and the battle, banished

past the threshold
of my room, rumbles
down the hall,
another door
slams—it is done.
                School impossible,
I skip the bus the next day,
call the dog
for a pre-dawn walk.
For once, she keeps close—
I touch her coarse
warmth, chance to meet
her eyes: the usual unnerving
stare squinches to a smize.
I scratch above her brow:
a cloud of dust lifts
with my fingertips.
We take off running
along the ridge, then down
trails grown restive with sumac,
its twining red tendrils.
Christmas trees sprout
beyond the barbed boundary—
the real crop is weed,
tucked beneath. Unseen
by people or sun, we are shadows
slipping 'round trees,
dust devils behind us, and before us
gleam more poison
oak leaves—their sentinel red
lines the path, sloping low
to the creek, its parched

bed littered with stones.
The valley is dark.
Heavy tread down
to crouch at the bed-edge
of no-river—
there I dig fingers in, find
a meanness of mind,
pelt small rocks at bigger.
Between bitter ramparts
and blackberry briars—
mind full of stone,
multitude of stones—
hit a boulder where
juts its chin, mouth
lost to moss.
            Then rising from the litter
of rocks, I run the hillside
the hard way, on its no-path
of wedded root and rock.
The mountain is steep.
Slips and tears, then up
gasps the overlook, its dark
hulk of boulder. There
climbs this lithe,
little body, a long-ago
girl, embracing
abrasion, its permanent,
granitic etch on jeans.
Frayed seams
unravel in the uncivil
forest. She holds fast
before the sun

shoulders up:
arrayed on the rock
like a quiver
of dropped spears,
ever-sharpening,
hardening to cure.
            But the heart run so far
from its home-hollow
stumbles, stutters
against rib rails.
A girl now descending
from stone face plunges
the profusion of thorns
for mean pleasures:
black, dusty fruits.
She stumbles through to a clearing
of redwoods and stream bed—
between the tree towers
morning drifts in, silent, dusty,
and orange.
            The memory of music
lofts arms, fingertips
slick-snap as dust
lifts, falls. In the spinning
she hums a no-song
of goodness now gone,
paean to forgetfulness,
scenes of gratuitous badness—
a berry-hennaed handmaiden
of loneliness and dirt.
The dog sits and pants.
            In time, the frame slips—

she's out again, tearing
through overgrowth
of thistle, poison oak,
and yellow-flecked broom,
heedless of all
posted warnings. The world
is unsettled, flickering:
between trees, morning bursts:
then a hill brings back night.
            Dog at my heels,
I pick through false oak,
back to the barb-rung
ridge road, shadowed
by a near hill; dim, dry,
dust-clouded as usual,
and my eyes, my mouth—
my tongue rolls the grit
and teeth grind it—
hating this place.
Wanting it gone.
Wanting it done, the
wanting of something
all my own.
            The dog halts, ears up.
Just a short way from home,
in an untended thicket,
a primitive head
lifts, unblinking,
from its coils—
the dog gathers,
ready to strike—
fear wraps

round my feet.
The blood-beat
thuds. Quick
glance: a rough rock—
I could reach it
if I am careful and slow.
The tiled wedge hovers.
I could smash
its lovely, blank eyes
to jelly, wreck
its perfect,
mottled flesh. It holds
its beaded bracelet
high, as if a grace note,
suspended.
A slight tremor
in my hand, weight
of imagined stone—
the snake flicks, tastes
our presence
and coming day, ready to unfurl
its dumb innocence.
The dog twitches, feints—
No! Low-voiced,
but urgent—
bizarrely, she complies,
but for how long?
The promise of violence
surges—my hand
grips, releases.
Sweat springs.
The blood-drum beats.

I am ready.
Above, the world opens wide
its all-seeing, yellow eye.
I slowly bend
for jagged stone—
the rattler uncoils, sways
side to side, its dull
body brightening
in the unfolding swath of light—
turns
in a skin-slip
through grass,
vanishes
in the underbrush
like a whispered
Shhhh . . .
The dog lunges—
I grab her collar.
But I am shaking
as I kneel and wrap my arms
around her chest.
I don't know if I regret
not having struck
when I had the chance.
We turn back, spend the day
among the rocks and fallen oak
leaves and dust spirals,
chasing quail, running
away—always away—
from the ranch house.
            But Harley—
he nickers and stamps.

He's kept his shine—
my days fighting dust
and all its undoings
have left him red-coated,
gleaming, and fine.
But the season is high
for halter breaking.
          Late in the day I return
to a tangle of ropes
in the paddock twisting round
horse and Eric. Deborah
and Mom at the rails,
watching. Deborah's
shouted taunts
like ropes meant to truss—
Show that little shit
what a man can do!
          I join the women, staring
at Eric's broad back,
taut, as criss-crossing cords
pull my horse, his head
webbed in insistent
nylon—*not there! Here!*
demand ropes and halter.
Harley's reply
his dirt-scrubbed hide,
scuffed legs snaked
with confusion—lassos,
leads tight, pulling tighter.
So *this* is how it's done?
The horse's neck stretching
up, head out—

like taffy, to be pulled
and molded, made pliable
and sweet. Harley
sticks his bubblegum
body to ground, head bound
to line, yoked
to the pacing, grunting,
hard-swearing man.
Face reddening
as if doused with wine,
Eric jerks Harley's head
around back, and farther,
in just the way a neck shouldn't:
sinews stretch,
he groans, eyes roll
to whites—inflamed,
the man's got him
by the jaw.
            But a pall leaches
Eric's face—now a mask,
rage-clenched. He drags
the once-red body
like doomed, incensed
Achilles dragged
Hector into filth—
worked a body to meat
suited only for a dog.
            Still won't stand.
Eric grabs a colt-hoof,
ropes a leg, pulls this way,
then that, yanks,
then a blood-yelp: *Damn!*

Damn damn fool horse—!
Dust raised. Not beast.
Harley's side is heaving
in the heat; he trembles
beneath his armor
of passivity, immovable,
obeisant only to gravity.
Eric gasps, drops to his knees.
Down. Farther down. Give way,
man, hands upon ground. Head bowed.
No sweat remains to pacify
the dust plumes, no appeasing
those bitchy catcalls beyond the paddock.
            Released, both creatures
sink into the gift of one man's grief.
Eric, panting, buries his face—
his hands' cradle a tomb
of one man's battles
I won't uncover.
            Harley heaves a great sigh, stretches
his dust-encrusted body,
all ropes now gone slack—relaxes, settles
somehow lower in the ground,
groans,
exhales, his once-burnished being
now coated with dirt.
            Legs lift. The horse
begins to roll, turns
with a grunt.
Dust heaves,
settles. He rests
a moment, flicks

an ear, dirt-caked.
Again: legs lift.
Cascades of earth
fall, dapple hide—
beneath, the jester
still—contrary,
brilliant chestnut,
cloaked in ash.
The fading light refracts—
a thousand temporary suns
begin to burn, the mountain
re-made in fire. The horse
sighs, again turns,
frees fells of earth
to red-smeared sky.
            When I was ten,
I left
my father to his smoke
and silence, lived
on a mountain
with my mother, left
Skyline Ranch
by a narrow track.
I left a dog, turning
Black Road switchbacks, left
horses, left the dark-
mantled mountain, left
Eric and Deborah, twisting
down, left my colt
in the night's open field.
I left
my colt

to his turning
and returned
to the flatlands,
like an empty bottle
rolling 'round
a lot of nothing at its center.
What wouldn't I do
now to make my heart
a wide cathedral—
so open to forgiveness—
that no one who entered
could ever leave.

L. Myers (b.1974)
Faded photos and scribblings, yellowed and torn

Pulled together into an impossibly seamless whole

The Cherry Tree

Almost forgotten, how it leans
in the sun's failing breath—the best kind
of forgetfulness, finding
what has slipped
your mind climbs back
into the painting. Figures
in gloss of limb
steal in
the scene, seem to glow.

Brushed in mottled blue,
perhaps floral, the girl's dress
must be lifting, falling,
like a sonnet about her knees
as she ascends
the ladder, stretches
for the last summer fruit. So much
branching beyond
the frame—the cherries
now almost out of sight. The landscape
remains unchanged, but the light
falls now differently on the page.

Climbing down to plain grass—
so many worlds have already fallen
around you, unnoticed.

One would never know how long
the chorus of round vowels will continue to tumble
to the shadowed green.

It is growing late.

You've come so far in-
to the trees, forgotten paint,
canvas—whatever original
intention lies behind the scene,
you must choose
your preferred shadows, walk in
tangled shade.

Balthus (1908–2001)
The Cherry Tree, 1940

Despite everything, cherries

Notes

GALLERIES 1 AND 3

Many of the poems in these sections reference or bear the titles of paintings by Balthus. Consulted sources include Damian Pettigrew's documentary film *Balthus Through the Looking-Glass* (1996); Nicolas Fox Weber's August 29, 1999 article in *The New Yorker*, "The Balthus Enigma"; Sabine Rewald's catalogue from the September 2013 to January 2014 Balthus exhibition at the Metropolitan Museum of Art, *Balthus: Cats and Girls: Paintings and Provocations* (2013); Guy Davenport's *A Balthus Notebook* (The Ecco Press, 1989); and Stephen Dobyns's *The Balthus Poems* (Scribner, 1982), as well as various other interviews, articles, and books.

The Blanchard Children

The disposition of Picasso's estate, which included this painting, resembled the "Cubist construction" of Picasso's own family, as described by writer Deborah Trustman: "wives, mistresses, legitimate and illegitimate children . . . and grandchildren—all strung on an axis like the backbone of a figure with unmatched parts." See "The Battle for Picasso's Multi-Billion-Dollar Empire" by Milton Esterow, *Vanity Fair,* March 7, 2016.

Still Life

The gallery tag includes a slightly modified quotation of John Russell's review of the 1984 Balthus show at the New York Met, which appeared in *The New York Times* on February 19, 1984, section 2, page 31 in the Art View section under the headline, "Balthus Mesmerizes With His Chilling Imagery."

The Victim

The encounter between artist and model in the poem is my invention. After Balthus left Paris to fight in the war, Thérèse and Balthus did not meet again. Balthus completed *La Victime* upon his return to Paris after the war. The model is unknown, but the face is clearly (to me, anyway) that of Thérèse, perhaps based on earlier sketches. The quote, "The past remains within us, an affliction," is from Ted Morgan's interview with Balthus, published as "Balthus Receives a Visitor," *The New York Times,* January 9, 1994. Thérèse died of unknown causes in 1950. She was twenty-five.

The Guitar Lesson
The poem modifies excerpts from interviews with Balthus, especially Richard Gere's September 1, 2001 conversation with Balthus in *The Art Newspaper*.

GALLERY 2

As Jay DeFeo Paints *Deathrose/The White Rose/The Rose* (1958–66)
The line, "And the whole thing commenced from a scratch," quotes Jay DeFeo. That quotation, and other indirectly influential material, can be found in the Archives of American Art Oral History interview with Jay DeFeo, June 3, 1975–January 23, 1976.

The line, "*like walking on the back of a whale*," quotes Bruce Conner, from the essay "In the Heat of *The Rose*" by Bill Berkson.

Additional sources consulted include *Jay DeFeo: A Retrospective* by Dana Miller and the Jay DeFeo Retrospective at the Whitney Museum of American Art, February 28 to June 2, 2013. This piece (and other pieces in this collection) are also in conversation with John Hollander's *The Gazer's Spirit: Poems Speaking to Silent Works of Art* (University of Chicago Press, 1985).

Pop Art No. 5
Baroque Vase, Harry Myers Jr.'s controversial ceramic sculpture, was shown in Seattle in the late '50s or early '60s. LaMar Harrington mentions the incident with the school kids in *Ceramics of the Pacific Northwest* (University of Washington Press, 1979). She also quotes part of Harry's presentation at the Fourth National Conference of the American Craftsmen's Council at the University of Washington in 1961, where he argued against the distinction between "fine arts" and "crafts."

Harry maintained that ceramics should be considered a major art form in its own right: "Creation should be no different in clay than in paint." His view was controversial at the time, and especially in the then-conservative Seattle area, as was Harry's "visceral, risk-taking" work. Both perhaps had something to do with his being fired from his teaching position at the University of Washington Department of Art. Harry returned to the more welcoming California Bay Area atmosphere in 1965 to teach at California State University at Hayward.

The ceramic sculpture referred to as "*Heap*" in this piece was shown and catalogued as *Pouch Form.* But we called it "*Heap*" or "*Pile*" or "*Cow Pile.*"

On "Elizabeth Bishop and the Management of Distance"
This piece is built around the complete text of Elizabeth Bishop's poem "Cirque d'Hiver."

GALLERY 3

The Other Horse in *Andrei Rublev*
This poem refers to a scene of a Tatar invasion of a village in Tarkovsky's film *Andrei Rublev.* A horse tumbles down the stairs and appears to fall on a spear. To produce the scene, the horse was first shot in the neck and pushed down the stairs. After being speared, the horse was shot in the head. In a 1967 interview, Tarkovsky said, "we took the horse from the slaughterhouse. If we didn't kill her that day, she would have been killed the next day in the same way. We did not think up any special torments, so to speak, for the horse."

Perspective with a Pen
The second and third sections of this poem borrow from Daniele Barbaro's *La pratica della perspettiva* (The Practice of Perspective), 1568. Barbaro describes his invention of the *camera obscura*, a method of projecting images from life onto paper. The invention was intended to aid artists in creating drawings that were more accurate to reality. The original text (in translation) is reproduced on the

website "Molecular Expressions: Science, Optics & You" as follows:

> Close all shutters and doors until no light enters the camera except through the lens, and opposite hold a piece of paper, which you move forward and backward until the scene appears in the sharpest detail. There on the paper you will see the whole view as it really is, with its distances, its colours and shadows and motion, the clouds, the water twinkling, the birds flying. By holding the paper steady you can trace the whole perspective with a pen, shade it and delicately colour it from nature.

The third, fourth, and fifth sections of this poem refer to the uncut prologue of Tarkovsky's film *Andrei Rublev* (1966), which contains a transfixing slow-motion scene of a horse rolling on the ground. In another, later scene, a primitive hot air balloon and its pilot crash to the ground. The same horse walks past the smoking crash and out of the scene.

Unfortunately, the original film release cut the scene of the rolling horse to only a few seconds and elided much of the crash scene, which eliminates the time-dilating beauty of the slow-motion rolling of the horse, and obfuscates the ironic contrast between the fallen pilot and machine on the one hand, and the living, untethered horse on the other.

Acknowledgments

Thanks are due to the following journals, where these poems first appeared (sometimes in different versions):

The American Journal of Poetry: "*Summertime* (2010) in Slemani" and "The Other Horse in *Andrei Rublev*"
California Quarterly: "*The Cherry Tree*"
The Ekphrasis Review: "*The Blanchard Children,*" "*Still Life,*" "*Thérèse sur une banquette,*" "*La Victime,*" and "*Thérèse*"
LIT Magazine: "As Jay DeFeo Paints *Deathrose/The White Rose/The Rose*"
New Verse Review: "At the Window"
One: "The Triangular Field"
Shadowgraph Magazine: "On 'Elizabeth Bishop and the Management of Distance' "
Southern Indiana Review: "*Young Girl at the Window*"
The Southern Review: "Mother, 1975"

Earlier versions of several poems in this collection were published in *Regards to Balthus*, a limited-edition chapbook (Seven Kitchens Press, 2023).

Thank you to Farrar, Straus and Giroux for permission to use Elizabeth Bishop's poem "Cirque d'Hiver."

About the Author

Lenore Myers was born to artist parents who tried to live as semi-bohemians in the suburbs. When that fell apart, the author spent her childhood and youth moving between different towns in Northern California. After spending more years moving around the United States and abroad, she returned to the greater Bay Area to be near family while raising her son. Her chapbook, *Regards to Balthus*, was published by Seven Kitchens Press in 2023. Her poems and essays appear in a variety of literary journals.

Sixteen Rivers Press is a shared-work, nonprofit poetry collective dedicated to providing an alternative publishing avenue for San Francisco Bay Area poets. Founded in 1999 by seven writers, the press is named for the sixteen rivers that flow into San Francisco Bay.

SAN JOAQUIN • FRESNO • CHOWCHILLA • MERCED • TUOLUMNE
STANISLAUS • CALAVERAS • BEAR • MOKELUMNE • COSUMNES • AMERICAN
YUBA • FEATHER • SACRAMENTO • NAPA • PETALUMA